Anonymus

Reception by the clergy and laity of Baltimore, Washington and Georgetown

Anonymus

Reception by the clergy and laity of Baltimore, Washington and Georgetown

ISBN/EAN: 9783741178641

Manufactured in Europe, USA, Canada, Australia, Japa

Cover: Foto ©Thomas Meinert / pixelio.de

Manufactured and distributed by brebook publishing software
(www.brebook.com)

Anonymus

Reception by the clergy and laity of Baltimore, Washington and Georgetown

Anonymus

Reception by the clergy and laity of Baltimore, Washington and Georgetown

RECEPTION

BY THE

CLERGY AND LAITY

OF

Baltimore, Washington and Georgetown,

OF HIS GRACE,

The Most Rev. Archbishop Spalding,

On his Return from the Council of the Vatican:

WITH

THE RESOLUTIONS AND PROTESTS AGAINST THE SACRILEGIOUS
INVASION OF ROME AND THE PAPAL STATES.

———————

BALTIMORE:
PUBLISHED BY JOHN MURPHY & CO.
Printers to the Pope, and to the Archbishop of Baltimore.
182 BALTIMORE STREET.
1870.

INTRODUCTION.

THERE is always, even in the worst and darkest
times, enough truth among men to flood the world
with light and fill all hearts with gladness. We cannot refrain from giving utterance to this thought, this
cheering conviction when we recall the welcome-home
extended on Thursday, November 10th, 1870, to a
venerable fellow-citizen and beloved Christian Bishop;
in a word, to one of the men whom, in a magnificent
hymn of her liturgy, the Catholic Church styles the
real friends of mankind and true lights of the world:

ET VERA MUNDI LUMINA.

This little volume, made up almost entirely of
the different reports placed before the public by the
Press the morning after that cordial reception, is
designed to be the history, in a more permanent form,
of a day that in years to come will be remembered
as one of the brightest in the annals of the American Church, and one of the most honorable to the
City of Baltimore. It is also intended to be a record
of the generous sympathy with which men of almost
every creed and country, no matter how divergent
their politics, shared the joy of their Catholic fellow-
countrymen. No one can read the various accounts,
and note the kindly tone, the eloquent thoughts and
language of journals whose influence on public opinion
no man doubts, and not be reminded of the famous

line of the old heathen poet, which nearly two thousand years ago electrified a Roman audience and shook the theatre with thunders of applause:

" Homo sum : humani nihil á me alienum puto."
(I am a man : whate'er belongs to man, comes home to me.)

The noble sentiment touched a chord which, we trust, will never be found wanting in the heart of the American people. For if out of the strange, multifarious elements that now commingle in American society, one great, homogeneous nation, is ever to arise and fulfil the destiny which God has marked out for us on this Western continent, will it not be by the gradual growth and development of such elements of fraternal concord and mutual confidence as this public demonstration, with all its attendant circumstances, seems to us to have admirably exemplified. But let abler pens than our's fill up the details of this happy day, and show some cause for believing that not always nor altogether true is the adage: "politicians neither love nor hate."

We subjoin the account of a similar demonstration by the Catholics of Washington and Georgetown.

Arrival of Archbishop Spalding.

A MAGNIFICENT RECEPTION—FIFTY THOUSAND PEOPLE ON THE STREETS
—A GRAND PROCESSION—THE ARRIVAL AT THE CATHEDRAL—RE-
CEPTION BY THE SEMINARIANS—THE WELCOME AND THE RESPONSE
—SERVICES IN THE CATHEDRAL—ADDRESS TO AND RESPONSE OF
THE ARCHBISHOP—PROTEST AGAINST THE INVASION OF ROME BY
ITALY, &C., &C.

Yesterday, says the Baltimore Gazette, was a day long to be remembered by the people of Baltimore. It has rarely occurred that so
many left their homes to give welcome to the occupant of any position,
either civil or ecclesiastical. It had been announced since Tuesday morning that His Grace, the Most Reverend Archbishop of Baltimore, had
reached New York, en route from Rome, and would be in Baltimore at
half past three o'clock on Thursday afternoon. It was naturally expected
that the entire Catholic population would be ready to greet him, but
the result showed that thousands of others, early yesterday afternoon,
from every quarter of the city, had bent their steps to Broadway, until
that spacious thoroughfare, at three o'clock, was densely filled from
Baltimore street to Canton avenue.

Not only was the street filled, but the windows of all the houses on
both sides were thronged with people, and there was a general disposition to do honor to the venerable Prelate who, since his residence in
Baltimore and his administration of the Archdiocese, has made hosts
of friends by the purity of his life and the noble charities which he has
built up.

In the same kind spirit the Sunday Bulletin observed:

The return of the Most Rev. Archbishop Spalding to this city on
Thursday, after more than a year's absence in Rome, as a member of
the Œcumenical Council, was signalized with more than ordinary
religious ceremony and marks of personal respect. The venerable Prelate, alike distinguished for his learning as a scholar, and devoutness
and zeal as an exalted Christian pastor, is held in the most affectionate
esteem by the faithful of his diocese, and has the utmost personal
regard of our citizens irrespective of religious sect. His return to our

midst is no ordinary event, with those especially over whom he governs, and his presence will infuse a gladness into the hearts of many who look upon him with a peculiar religious filial regard.

The Most Rev. Archbishop was, perhaps, the greatest representative of the Catholic Church of America in the Œcumenical Council. In that body—the largest and most splendid assemblage of talent and wisdom the Church has ever known—he was assigned a high position of responsibility, and dignified it by his varied learning and ripened judgment. The associate of the wisest, the most accomplished, and the most exalted dignitaries of the Catholic world, his name was always conspicuous in advancing the work of his office, and realizing results satisfactory to the eminent authorities who had designated him for it. Arduous as his labors have been, advanced as he is in years, and bowed down somewhat by the mutations and reverses in the temporal supremacy of the Pontifical power, of which he and millions of his persuasion were defenders, he returns to resume his Archiecopiscopal functions, as we learn, in good health, and with no terrors upon that zeal which has always been his great and prominent characteristic. Beloved by all, he is a worthy recipient of all the honors that were paid to him.

The safe arrival in New York, says the Baltimore Sun, a few days since, of the Most Reverend Archbishop Spalding, of the archdiocese of Baltimore, on his return from an extended sojourn in Rome as a member of the Œcumenical Council, naturally excited much interest among the Catholic community of Baltimore, and begat active measures to give him a fitting reception home, culminating yesterday, on the occasion of his reaching this city, in an ovation of which any crowned head of Europe might well feel proud. The Archbishop, distinguished alike for his scholarship and his kindly spirit as a man, and for his Christian zeal as the head of his Church in America, is deservedly popular in the community in which he resides, and the demonstration of yesterday is but an evidence of the deep hold the eminent Prelate has on the affections of his people. The arrangements for the reception were hastily made within the past few days, but in the hands of competent committees and the chief marshalship of Dr. R. H. GOLD-SMITH, they were admirably carried out, and the entire affair was a grand success, all the Catholic societies and the clergy and other officials of that denomination taking part therein. The Archbishop returns in greatly improved health, and in passing along the route of procession was quick in observing and recognizing the faces of old and numerous friends.

THE GATHERING ON BROADWAY.

As early as 2 P. M. crowds of men, women and children commenced assembling on Broadway, and by the time the whistle announced the coming of the train, that wide and handsome thoroughfare from Baltimore street as far south as the Broadway Institute was alive with human beings. In the meantime the different associations which had assembled at their usual meeting places had arrived and taken position in line, the right resting on Baltimore street, and the left extending several squares below Bank street. The members of the societies were formed in open order, so that the Archbishop and the special Committee of Reception might pass in review. The committee were early on the spot in barouches, and consisted of Judge T. P. Scott, Judge B. D. Danels, Messrs. T. C. Jenkins, Wm. Kennedy, John W. Jenkins, Joseph Kreutzer, Esqs., and Hon. J. Thompson Mason. Father H. B. Coskery, Vicar-General of the Archdiocese of Baltimore, and a large number of the Reverend Clergy, were also in attendance in carriages.

A TRIUMPHAL ARCH.

A triumphal arch was thrown across about one-half of the wide avenue at the intersection of Bank street, opposite St. Patrick's church. It was beautifully decorated with natural flowers and evergreens, and bore in large letters the inscription, "The Children of St. Patrick Welcome their Beloved Archbishop," and also " Cead Mille Faitha." Beneath this arch and on each side of it were stationed some three hundred of the female pupils of St. Patrick's school, neatly attired in white, and each bearing in her hand a bouquet. The picture presented was very pleasing.

ARRIVAL OF THE ARCHBISHOP.

The train reached Broadway promptly on time, and as soon as he and his friends alighted a most cordial greeting was extended by Father Coskery and the gentlemen of the Committee of Reception. The Archbishop was conducted to a superb open coach drawn by four fine horses, where he was seated with Bishop Becker, Father Coskery, and Judge Scott, amid hearty cheers from the large crowd in the locality. A volley of artillery was fired from an adjacent height, the bells of St. Patrick's and St. Michael's Churches, in the immediate vicinity, the Cathedral, and in fact all the Catholic Churches of the city, pealed forth, and amid the greatest enthusiasm the party was driven slowly beneath the arch and up the line, the members of the various associations uncovering, as did also those in the coach, the Archbishop bowing to either side in recognition of demonstrations. From many windows on Broadway flags were displayed, ladies waved their handkerchiefs, all of which the Archbishop with his keen eye appeared to take in from point to point, gallantly, with uncovered head, making his acknowledgments. On reaching Baltimore street, at the head of Broadway, the coach containing the Archbishop was halted, and the entire procession passed before him in review, those composing the line saluting him as they passed to take position in the escort.

THE PROCESSION.

The procession moved up Baltimore street in the following order: Platoon of Policemen; the Chief Marshal, DR. H. R. GOLDSMITH, and MICHAEL MULLIN and F. X. WARD as Aids, all mounted. First Division, Chief Marshal J.A. OSTENDORF, with L. H. Wieman and Henry Cashmyer as Assistants; band of music; the American and the Papal flags; St. Michael's Beneficial Society, Fer. Amend, Marshal, 40 men, with a Papal flag and banner, having on it a likeness of the patron saint of the society; St. Joseph's German Beneficial Society, with green banner, with figure of the saint in the act of blessing a child, about 50 men; St. Stephen's Beneficial Society, N. Close, Marshal, 30 strong, with handsome banner; St. Peter's Beneficial Society, 50 strong, Fred. Nugent, Marshal, with elegant silk banner; St. Aloysius' Society, Augustus Hessler, Marshal, 100 men, wearing blue and white sashes, with banner and American flag; St. Alphonsus' Society of St. Michael's Church, 50 men, with American flag; St. John's Beneficial Society; St. James' Beneficial Society; St. Martinus' Beneficial Society, Wm. H. Hanson, Marshal, 30 strong; the Society of the Holy Cross; St. Martin's Beneficial Society, and delegations from a number of others.

The Second Division followed, JOHN T. PIQUETT, Chief Marshal, with Patrick Reilly and M. E. McMahon, assistants. Band of Music: Saint Patrick's Beneficial Society, Michael Ward, Marshal, with American flag and beautiful silk banner, bearing a likeness of St. Patrick surrounded by appropriate emblems; Sons of St. Patrick Beneficial Society, Henry McSweeney, Marshal, 80 men, carrying a beautiful silk banner, having on it the figure of a female with infant in arms, and on the reverse the name of the Association, established 1865; the Hibernian Society, Patrick Reilly, Marshal, 125 men, and headed by the Ninth Regiment Band, and carrying their elegant large silk banner, just renovated by Sisco Brothers, bearing on it a well executed likeness of St. Patrick, surmounted with the motto "Erin go Bragh," beneath an inscription in Irish characters, translated "St. Patrick, Pray for Us," on the reverse side the green sunburst of Ireland, a picture of the Maid of Erin resting on her harp, with dog watching at her feet; the Father Mathew's Temperance Society of St. Joseph's Parish, Frederick Burrows, Marshal, 80 men, headed by Winter's Fifth Regiment Band, and carrying a large green flag; the Students of Rock Hill College, Ellicott City, 50 strong, with the College Band, and accompanied by Brother Bettelin, the President of the College, and others of the Christian Brotherhood ; St. Bridget's Beneficial Society, Martin T. Raftery, Marshal, 60 men; St. Ignatius' Society, M. S. McMahon, Marshal, 150 men, with handsome silk banner; St. John the Evangelist Beneficial Society ; Beneficial Society of the Immaculate Conception, Bernard Linn, Marshal, 50 men, with beautiful banner, having on it the figure of the Blessed Virgin in the attitude of prayer; St. Ignatius' Beneficial Society.

The Third Division was marshaled by JOSEPH S. HEUISLER, aided by Edward Jenkins and C. F. Farnan—Band of Music; 200 boy pupils from St. John's School, 200 from St. Vincent's, 350 from St. Alphonsus', 200 from St. Peter's and 200 from the Immaculate Conception, all accompanied by their teachers; the members of the Christian Brotherhood ; a Papal flag; a guard of honor, consisting of one delegate from each Association in the Procession ; the Band from Fort McHenry, Prof. Vitt ; two open barouches, containing the Committee of Reception ; coach and four with the Archbishop and companions. Then followed the members of the Young Catholics' Friend Society in strong force, acting as a special guard of honor, and then the boys from St. Mary's Industrial School, in plain gray dress, to the number of over one hundred.

A long line of open barouches and carriages, containing the Reverend Clergy and distinguished Catholic citizens, closed the procession. Among the former were the Right Rev. Bishop BECKER, of Wilmington, Delaware ; Rev. Fathers C. I. WHITE, J. A. WALTER, Rev. P. F. McCARTHY and Rev. JAS. McDEVITT, of Washington, D. C.; Rev. Father DUBREUL, Superior of the Theological Seminary of St. Sulpice, Baltimore, and Rev. Mr. FERTE, President of St. Charles' College, near Ellicott City.

THE LINE OF MARCH.

The line of march was up Baltimore street to Charles, and thence to Mulberry and. Cathedral. On Charles street, near Lexington, a large piece of canvas was stretched across the street, under which the Procession passed, which bore the words "Welcome Home." Along the entire route much interest was manifested, the sidewalks, as well as windows and doors, being filled with spectators, who gave tokens to the Archbishop of recognition, which were constantly reciprocated. Besides the flags in Broadway, many others were displayed along the route, and ladies continued to give expression of their pleasure in welcoming the venerable prelate by waving of handkerchiefs, &c., and the whole Catholic community gave evidence of their joy in receiving home

once more their esteemed and highest ecclesiastic. When the head of
the Procession reached the Cathedral-street entrance to the Cathedral
the line again took position in open order, and the Archbishop and
others in carriages passed up and alighted in front of the edifice.

AT THE CATHEDRAL.

Previous to the arrival of the Procession at the Cathedral the streets
in that vicinity, together with the enclosure of the building, were well
filled with persons eager to obtain a glance at their devoted Archbishop.
No one was admitted into the church edifice but the regular congregation or, holders of pews until the mass meeting was held, when the
doors were thrown open to all. The students of the Theological Seminary of St. Sulpice, 70 in number, together with a large number of the
clergy of the Archdiocese and visiting clergy from other sections of the
country were ranged upon the northern portico of the Cathedral
anxiously awaiting the arrival of the Archbishop. Upon the arrival of
his Grace he was escorted from his carriage to the steps of the edifice
by Judge SCOTT and Judge DANELS, where he put on his Pontifical
robes, assisted by Rev. Fathers COSKERY and DOUGHERTY. Immediately after the Archbishop had robed, Judge J. T. MASON stepped
forward and delivered the following address of welcome on behalf of
the laity :

"Most Reverend Archbishop : The best mode we can adopt, and, I
am sure, the one most agreeable to yourself, to express our gratification
in welcoming you to your friends and your home, is to render thanks
to our Great Father in Heaven, He 'who hath measured the waters in
the hollow of His hand,' for having been with you upon the mighty
deep, and preserved you from the perils of the sea ; and, much more to
be thankful for, for having endowed you with wisdom, with courage and
with faith in maintaining the Eternal Truth in the great Council of
God's elect. You return with the approval of your own conscience,
with the special benediction of the Holy Father, and with the applause
of the faithful throughout the world.

"Though distant land and seas separated you from those who now
look upon your face once more with emotions of gratification and joy,
you, perhaps, do not realize the extent to which you have been cher-
ished in their hearts and remembered in their prayers during the long
and wearisome hours of your absence.

"The reception which is to-day extended to you is not only an honor
and a triumph, but it is intended as a reward justly due to noble and
pious works. No hero returning from worldly achievements could merit
more than you do human applause and human honors. Few saints return-

ing from labors of love and pious sacrifices better deserve the grateful tears and the tribute of thanks from the holy and just. No one could bring home from abroad, for the benefit of his friends, nobler and more priceless trophies than those which now cluster around your character and services.

"But, if I properly appreciate the temper and disposition of those who now surround you, I can affirm that for neither of these purposes are we here to-day. We come to welcome neither the great champion of truth nor the hero who has braved the tempest and the sea, nor he who has left the impress of his vigorous mind upon one of the most important, as it will be one of the most enduring pages of the world's history, nor to congratulate you upon your new ecclesiastical honors; but we come in the spirit of that simple love and affection which prompts little children to meet and welcome with outstretched arms a father whose long absence made their home cheerless and desolate, and whose return brings joy and gladness. We come to receive a father's blessings, to conduct you once more to your old familiar seat in the midst of a devoted household, and again to resume those tender and affectionate relations which have endeared us to you, more even than the honor and dignity which attach to your character as Prelate.

"There is but one shadow that falls across the sunlight of the Catholic's joy on this occasion, and that is the reminder which your Grace's person suggests of the present unhappy condition of the temporal kingdom of that just man made perfect, the Holy Father, the Pope. But if ours be the Church of God, as our faith teaches, why need we fear or despond under any trial? What are the kingdoms and powers of earth compared with His kingdom and His power? He has said through His prophet, 'Behold the nations are as a drop of a bucket, and are counted as the small dust of the balance. Behold He taketh up the isles as a very little thing. He bringeth the princes to nothing; He maketh the judges of the earth as vanity.'

"Let us rest in the hope that early He will redeem His promise, and that He will soon restore the Head of the Church to his legitimate powers. Although this good man's sun on earth is nearly set; although he walks upon the solemn, silent shores of eternity, about to embark upon its waters, yet may his life be spared long enough to enable him

' To heal Rome's harms, and wipe away her woe.'

"We need not, in conclusion, assure you in words how glad we are to see you once more at home and in our midst. The thousand tearful eyes that are now looking upon your venerable person; the hands that are impatient to extend their cordial grasp; the hearts that throb with

2

filial affection to receive your blessing, all tender to you, more eloquently than words can express, an affectionate greeting and sincere welcome."

In response to Judge MASON's address Archbishop SPALDING replied as follows:

THE ARCHBISHOP'S RESPONSE.

"Honorable Judge Mason and Dearly Beloved of the Laity of the Archdiocese of Baltimore:—I thank you from my heart for this cordial and sincere greeting, and expression of your kindly feelings towards me; I also thank you for endorsing my action in the Œcumenical Council, which is so well known to the clergy and laity that it needs no defense from me. I am sincerely proud of my children of the laity of Baltimore here present, and of the great city of Baltimore, and I most heartily thank all here present for this ovation."

After the address a procession, composed of the students of St. Sulpice and the clergy, followed by the Most Rev. Archbishop, and Bishop BECKER, of Wilmington, Delaware, was formed, and preceded by a cross and incense bearer, moved up the main aisle of the church to the altar, during which the band of the Fourth Artillery, which was stationed in the choir, played a march. Arriving at the altar, which was tastefully decorated with natural flowers and lighted candles, the Archbishop knelt at his desk and engaged in silent prayer for a few minutes, when, arising, he proceeded to his throne. Following this, the Rev. Father COSKERY ascended the steps of the main altar on the epistle side, and read the prescribed prayers, after which the antiphon *Ecce Sacerdos Magnus* was sung by a number of the students.

Rev. Father COSKERY, in behalf of the clergy of the Archdiocese of Baltimore, then delivered the following address:

"Most Reverend Archbishop and Beloved Father: Your children, of both the clergy and laity, hail with rapturous delight the return of their Archbishop, of whom, assuredly, we have reason to be proud, if ever a devotedly attached flock had reason to be proud of their Prelate. The testimony of the Catholic world 'beareth witness' to our own testimony, and convinces us that we speak not merely the language of filial love, pride and partiality, but of truth, which will be historic when we assert that, amid the illustrious lights which shine so conspicuously in the great general Vatican Council, few have done more than our own Archbishop in the fulfilment of the episcopal office, to enlighten in the things of God 'every man that cometh into the world.'

"Most Reverend Archbishop: To use the language of your own letter, announcing your long desired return to the bosom of a devoted flock, 'the Council has been prorogued till better days.' 'Till better days,' for, truly may we say with the apostle, 'The days are evil.' 'The abomination of desolation (is seen) standing in the holy place.' A so-called king, whom we are ashamed to call Catholic, despising the warning voice of Jesus Christ, and not capable of learning wisdom from other silly potentates who have *gone* before him, is impious, senseless and selfish enough to dream of rearing a short-lived, ephemeral success upon the ruins of the Church of Christ.

"We know, Most Reverend and Beloved Father, and all the world knows, that the Vicar of Christ on earth has not on earth a more devoted son than is our own Most Reverend Father. Hence we deem this a fitting occasion to enter as we do now and here, our (powerless, it may be, yet) heartfelt, protest against the shameless injustice and brute violence of the King of Italy, who, if he persist in his sacrilegious, hypocritical and short-sighted course, will infallibly find, what he perhaps does not now believe, that there is truth in the words of Christ, who, speaking of the Church, under the simile of a stone, says : ' Whosoever shall fall upon this stone shall be bruised, and upon whomsoever it shall fall it will crush him to atoms.' "

The Reverend Prelate, after the address of Father Coskery, arose from his throne and spoke in substance as follows :

ADDRESS TO THE CLERGY.

"Most Reverend Administrator and Dearly Beloved of the Clergy : I have but to repeat what I said to the distinguished orator for the laity, I thank you for your approval of my course in the Council at Rome. I pursued that course because it was my duty, and as you are all familiar with my action at that time, it needs no explanation from me. When I was in the Council I was but as a drop in a river, as one among many. Dearly beloved, I thank you all for this kindly greeting ; I have loved you all very much, but now, after this testimonial of your esteem, must love you more than ever. But there is one whom we all love, Pius IX., who is a prisoner in the hands of his enemies. Availing himself of the unprotected state of the Papal dominions, that chief of the Florentine Government, Victor Emmanuel, sent an army of some 60,000 men against a defenseless old man, whom to know is to love. Therefore I acquiesced in the wish of many persons, to adopt appropriate resolutions on this occasion when this vast assembly greets me home.

"The King of Italy drove me, with hundreds of others, from Rome, all in the name of liberty. I hope every Catholic heart here present will leap with exultation, when the resolutions which are to be offered shall be read."

THE MASS MEETING.

A mass meeting was then organized by the election of the following officers: President—Hon. T. PARKIN SCOTT; Vice-Presidents—Judge J. T. MASON, WM. KENNEDY, CHAS. M. DOUGHERTY, THOS. C. JENKINS, C. OLIVER O'DONNELL, ALFRED JENKINS, Judge B. D. DANELS, DANIEL J. FOLEY, THOS. C. YEARLEY, CUMBERLAND DUGAN, CHAS. WILLIAMSON, ROBERT MICKLE, JNO. MALLOY, COL. MATTHEWS, and COL. BENZINGER; Secretaries, F. X. WARD and J. S. HUEISLER.

Judge SCOTT, in accepting the position of President, made a few remarks explanatory of the purposes of the meeting.

THE PREAMBLE AND RESOLUTIONS.

JOS. S. HUEISLER, Esq., Secretary, then read a preamble, with the following resolutions:

"We, the Catholics of the Archdiocese of Baltimore, in general meeting assembled, to the number of more than fifty thousand, in order to welcome the return from Rome of our beloved Archbishop, wish to avail ourselves of this impressive occasion to give expression, in the face of all Christendom, to our earnest, solemn, and unanimous protest against the late invasion of the Roman States by the Florentine Government, and this, our indignant protest, is grounded upon the following, among other weighty reasons:

"1. This forcible invasion was made in open violation of solemn treaties, guaranteeing the independence of the Sovereign Pontiff in the government of the small remnant of territory which had been left to him; and what increases its atrocious injustice is the additional circumstance, that the pusillanimous invaders ungenerously availed themselves of the misfortunes of France, their former best friend and ally, to carry out their wicked purpose of spoliation. Without any previous declaration of war; without assigning any reason for their high-handed act other than the pretended political exigencies of their position, which really meant nothing else but that of their own interests and self-aggrandizement; without any complaints against the Pontifical Government, the paternal mildness of which is known over the whole world, and which was acceptable to the great body of the people who lived under its gentle sway; without cause and against all right, these bold and unscrupulous men struck down by violence a small and helpless neighboring State, the oldest and the most legitimate in its rights of all European Governments. It was a triumph of might against right, of brute force against justice.

15

" 2. The guilt of sacrilege was superadded to that of injustice. The Papal territory has been regarded by all Christendom, for more than a thousand years, not only as neutral, but even as sacred soil, belonging to two hundred millions of Christians scattered over the whole world, and administered for their benefit by the Visible Head of the Church and the Common Father of all. It was held as a patrimonial estate, belonging to the whole family, which had come down in unbroken descent, and as an unquestioned inheritance, through more than thirty generations; and which was regarded by the general consent of nations and the settled jurisprudence of long centuries, as necessary for the free and independent exercise of the Primacy by the successive incumbents of the Pontifical office, which necessarily involved free intercourse with all Christendom, without the pressure of any preponderating political influence, or the possibility of any hostile political hindrance. To secure this necessary freedom of action, a small independent territory was sufficient, and accordingly that assigned to the Pontiff by the wisdom and piety of past ages and the disposition of Providence, was large enough to insure their liberty, but not so large as to exercise any great, much less preponderating political influence over other nations.

" 3. The principle which lies at the basis of this time-honored, world-wide jurisprudence, is precisely that which was subsequently adopted by the founders of our own great republic, who wisely ordained that a small independent district should be marked out and set apart from the territory of the States, exempt from all State influence and control, as the seat of the General Government, to be administered for the benefit of all.

" The District of Columbia is neutral, and, in some sense, sacred soil, belonging to no particular State, but the common property of all the States. This provision was wisely made, in order to render the action of the General Government free and untrammeled by particular State influence, which would necessarily have the tendency to hamper its action, and to beget mistrust as to its freedom.

" As between the District of Columbia in its relation to the United States, and the Papal territory in its relation to the United States of Christendom, the principle is the same, and the parallelism is complete; and if the States of Maryland and Virginia, or any other State or States, availing themselves of a crisis favorable to their purpose, should invade and hold forcible possession of the District of Columbia, in violation of our settled jurisprudence, and for their own selfish purposes, the indignation which would burst forth throughout the land would be but an echo of that which now breaks forth throughout all Christendom on account of the sacrilegious invasion of the Papal States.

" And our confidence in the sound good sense and even-handed justice of our fellow-citizens of all classes and denominations, is such, as to
inspire us with the fullest certainty that all fair and impartial men will
be drawn to sympathize with us in the calamity which has temporarily
befallen our Church in its Visible Head. In the nature of things, the
calamity can be but transitory, just as in the hypothetical invasion of
the District of Columbia. The United States of Chris'.endom will redress this grievance as promptly and as indignantly, as would the United
States of America redress the other in the parallel case.

" 4. Notwithstanding the specious and hypocritical professions of the
Florentine Government, and the sham of a *plebiscite* managed under
the influence of the bayonet, we have the very best reasons for believing
and knowing, that the invasion was not invited or approved of by the
larger and sounder portion of the Roman people, and that the Pontiff,
far from being free, is virtually and even really a prisoner in the hands
of his enemies; the leaders of whom are, at the same time, the enemies
of all truth, of all justice and of all religion: and that, finally, under the
sad circumstances of durance in which he is held, guarded at his very
palace gates by a hostile soldiery, he cannot have that free intercourse
with Christendom which his high and responsible office of Visible Head
of the Church, for feeding the sheep and lambs of the whole flock committed to him in the person of the blessed Peter, and for confirming his
brethren necessarily requires; and that the faithful throughout the
world can feel no confidence whatever that their communications to him
and his answers to them will pass free and unmolested. Men who have
violated all treaties and foresworn all faith are manifestly not to be
trusted, at least whenever their selfish interests are involved.

" 5. Rome is not only the centre of religion, but it is the sanctuary
of ancient and modern literature and art; and well-grounded fears are
entertained lest this sanctuary should be violated, and its precious
treasures scattered or destroyed by the ruthless invader. The indica-
tions in this direction have been already unfavorable, in spite of the
brief period of the occupation, and the future is lowering and gloomy.

" 6. But what we protest against, with still more energetic indignation,
is the open insult to all Christendom implied in the breaking up of the
great Vatican Council, and the virtual expulsion from the capital of
Christendom of Bishops, who had, at great expense and peril, convened
from all parts of the world, to assist at the solemn Assizes of the Church.
They could no longer hope to be able to assemble in peace and liberty
around their Chief, to deliberate with him on the great interests of the
Catholic Church; and hence no alternative was left them, but to return
suddenly to their distant sees, and none to the venerable Pontiff but to
suspend, with a sorrowing heart, the Vatican Council.

" For this outrage the Florentine Government will have to account with a world-wide and indignant Christendom. For these and other reasons we solemnly and indignantly unite with two hundred millions of Christians in protesting against the sacrilegious invasion of the Papal States by the Florentine Government. And,

"Whereas our Holy Father, Pius IX., on the 29th of June, 1868, the Feast of the Holy Apostles Peter and Paul, did issue his Bull of Convocation for the meeting of the Œcumenical Council of the Vatican, to be opened on the 8th day of December, 1869, in the city of Rome ; and,

" Whereas the said Council did assemble accordingly, and under the guidan?e of the Holy Ghost, proceeded quietly with the work appointed to be done until on or about the 20th day of September, in the year 1870, when the States of the Church were, without cause and without any previous declaration of war, invaded by the troops of a neighboring monarch, King Victor Emmanuel, and the Holy Father was made prisoner and his government overthrown by violence, and the authority of his Holiness usurped by the creatures of the invader:

" Now, we, the Catholics of the Archdiocese of Baltimore, having been called together to meet our dear Father in God, the Most Reverend MARTIN JOHN SPALDING, Archbishop of this Diocese, on his return to his flock after participating in the proceedings of said Council, deem the present a proper occasion to express our firm convictions in relation to the outrage perpetrated by King Victor Emmanuel as above stated.

"*Therefore Resolved*, That the said invasion of the Papal Territories and the overthrow of the Government of his Holiness and usurpation of his Sovereignty were and are against right and justice, in violation of the terms of the Convention of the 15th of September, 1864, between the Emperor of France and the said King Victor Emmanuel, and of good faith, and an outrage against the civilized world.

" *Resolved*, The circumstances of the case would justify the intervention of all Christian Governments in favor of the restoration of his Holiness to his Sovereign rights."

At the conclusion of the reading the resolutions were unanimously adopted by all present in the Cathedral rising in their seats, and raising up their right hands. At the same time the Protest and Resolutions were read from the steps of the Cathedral to the vast multitude outside, who likewise enthusiastically adopted them, by raising their hands.

CONCLUSION.

After the meeting, the Most Rev. Prelate ascended the main altar, and while the vast audience knelt he gave them the Papal Benediction, after which he descended to the throne and unrobed, the choir, under the leadership of Professor Gegan, singing the Magnificat. All the clergy in the sanctuary, with the theological students, together with a number of the laity, then went in order and saluted the Archbishop by kissing the ring on his right hand, and indulged in congratulations, while the main body of the audience left the church.

On entering the Episcopal residence, another reception was given the Archbishop by the pupils of St. Mary's Industrial School, who sang a hymn of welcome, and one of their number presented him with a neat little address, to which His Grace replied in happy language. The school then dispersed, and most of the clergymen left for their various parishes; and the Archbishop was left to enjoy the quiet of his home.

RECEPTION OF THE ARCHBISHOP AT LOYOLA COLLEGE.

Last night, November 29, at half past seven o'clock, says the Baltimore Gazette, was appointed for the reception of His Grace, the Most Rev. Archbishop SPALDING, at Loyola College. The hall of the College was thronged to its utmost capacity with ladies and gentlemen, and a band of music occupied the gallery. The place assigned to the Archbishop was immediately in front of the stage, and he was surrounded by the Reverend Clergy. Mayor BANKS was present, as was also Hon. T. PARKIN SCOTT, Hon. JNO. THOMSON MASON, WILLIAM P. PRESTON, Esq., and others. The stage was occupied by students of the College appointed to address the Archbishop. Addresses were made by A. Hill, John Fueri (in German.) Thomas Chapelle, Frank Willoughby, Frank Hambleton (in French.) James M. Kelly, John P. O'Neil, and Lewis M. Hastings (in Latin.) Rev. Father SOURIN, on the part of the College, then delivered the following address:

Most Rev. Archbishop, Most Respected and Beloved Father in God: Once more in the midst of your people; once more on the soil of Maryland, with whose fair renown your name, *clarum et venerabile nomen*, is now more than ever, and forever associated; once more in the "Land of the Sanctuary," the birthplace of that form of freedom which, next to the glorious liberty of the children of God, all true men of this and of every age justly regard as one of heaven's best gifts—*civil and religious liberty!* Once more in the midst of your flock, committed to your care by the illustrious successor of him who first heard from the Eternal Shepherd of our souls, as His immediate representative on earth, "Feed my lambs; feed my sheep"—a flock bound to your Grace by all the sacred ties of obedience, love, gratitude, veneration, which *bind your heart* to the heart and throne of our Holy Father and Sovereign Pontiff, Pius IX; a loyalty which, in these days of disaster and crime, have rendered the very thought of the Archbishop of Baltimore dear to the Vicar of Jesus Christ, and your presence a thousandfold dearer, not only to us, but to every Catholic in America. At such a moment, Most Reverend and Beloved Father, in what more appropriate language can we welcome you, than in the words with which St. John Chrysostom greeted the return of his venerable and heroic Bishop, the aged Flavian, from the city and Court of Constantinople, "Blessed be God! who has deigned to grant that we should spend this day with joy and gladness; who has also restored the Head to the body, and the shepherd to the sheep; the teacher to the disciples; the General to the soldiers; the High-priest to the priests. Blessed be God, who does superabundantly more than we ask or expect. For the loving God, who always surpasses our requests with great excess, has also given back to us our Father more quickly than any expectation could have anticipated."

Permit me, then, though in the midst of so many, more capable of the duty, far more worthy of the honor, to congratulate you on your safe return, in the name of my Catholic fellow-countrymen and fellow-citizens, to repeat again the welcome home which, by thousands, they have given you to your diocese and to your Episcopal city, with the earnest prayer that Heaven may strengthen your Grace more and more for the arduous duties of your sacred office.

Permit me, in the name of my Reverend brethren of every order and congregation, to bless the Father of Mercies and the God of all consolation, who, at the moment when the clouds of war hover over land and sea, has heard your petition, "May the almighty and merciful Lord conduct us into the way of peace and prosperity, and may the Angel Raphael accompany us on our journey, that in peace, safety and joy we may return to our own."

And, in the name of my brethren of the Society, still, as your Grace can bear witness, so often and in so many lands, the

Doom'd to death, but fated not to die,

permit me, on this cheering occasion, to renew the homage of our profound respect, of our filial attachment, and of our readiness, "corde magno et animo volenti," to serve the Church of God, of which your Grace is here the chief pastor, and as is due to one whom we can so justly hail our Father and our Friend.

When we recall the memorable scenes, the all-important events that have occurred since your departure last fall from this city for Rome and the Vatican Council, what other thoughts, what other emotions than those of joy, and gratitude, and confidence, and purest reverence can fill our hearts, when we know that we can greet you this evening in the very words of the Bishop and martyr, St. Cyprian, to the fearless confessors of the primitive Church: "Behold! the Heavenly dignity ha

3

been marked on you by the brightness of a year-long honor. As many as are your days, so many are your praises; as many as are the courses of the months, so many are the increases of your merits." Accept, then, once more, this humble testimonial of what, in union with their fellow-citizens and their fellow-students throughout loved and honored Maryland, the sons of Loyola feel, far more deeply than we can express. For years to come, may it be our happy lot, "*Te pastorem sequentes*" following thee, our pastor, to lighten by our fidelity the burden of accumulated care and labors which such dark days as these heap on the heads of God's chosen servants, that your Grace may journey on through the remaining years of life, always able to say with the royal Psalmist: "Thou hast given gladness into my heart. Thou hast given me the protection of Thy salvation, and Thy right hand hath held me up. Thy name, O God of Israel! be blessed forever."

In reply, the Most Rev. Archbishop addressed himself to the members of the Society of Jesus, the regular Clergy, and the young gentlemen of the College, all of whom he thanked for the too kindly greeting which they had given him. 'Not too kindly from their stand-point, but from his. He never felt so small as when he was in the Vatican Council, where there were so many superior to him in sanctity and learning. Some of the speakers had spoken of the liberty of Maryland. He was proud of Maryland, and if he was not born on Maryland soil his father and mother were. But he was like the dove which returned to the ark, and he came back because he belonged to Maryland.'

'They all loved liberty, and especially Maryland liberty. The so-called Liberals of Italy and France knew nothing of liberty, and are but a disgrace to the term. They have a notion that liberty means to take what does not belong to them. The first idea after the revolutionary movement was to drive out the Jesuits and the poor women who work for charity.' He spoke of the Roman College, one-half of which had been taken possession of by the invaders, and there was a cry for the whole of it. He also spoke of the prostitution of the press to advance the cause of infidelity. ' This is so different from what is seen in Maryland. Those people are as ignorant of liberty as some are of psalmody, and are but the followers of Marat and Robespierre.' The Archbishop spoke at length on the subject of liberty, and declared the United States the freest Government on the face of the earth.

After the reception, the Reverend Clergy conducted the Archbishop to the refectory, where a handsome supper was spread. For an hour after the removal of the cloth there was an interchange of sentiment, and all present appeared delighted to do honor to him who stands at the head of the Church in the United States. The occasion was one of great interest to all who participated.

Reception in Washington and Georgetown, D. C.

THE OVATION TO ARCHBISHOP SPALDING—IMMENSE OUTPOURING OF THE
PEOPLE—ENDORSEMENT OF THE ARCHBISHOP'S ACTION IN ROME—
THE SONS OF THE CHURCH RE-AFFIRM THEIR SPIRITUAL ALLEGIANCE
TO THE POPE—INTERESTING CEREMONIES AT ST. MATTHEW'S CHURCH
—ADDRESSES OF WELCOME, AND RESPONSE OF THE ARCHBISHOP—
HIS RECEPTION BY THE STUDENTS OF GEORGETOWN COLLEGE.

Thursday, November 24, 1870, says the Daily Patriot, will long be
remembered by the Catholic community of Washington for the cordial
reception which they extended to their venerable Archbishop, and as an
occasion upon which they unmistakably re-affirmed their allegiance to
the Pope as the head of the Church.

For a week past there has been a stir in Catholic circles, owing to
the announcement that Archbishop SPALDING, of Baltimore, would pay
a visit to this city in his official capacity. Meetings were held by the
different Catholic organizations and the members of the different parishes
throughout the city, subscriptions were raised, and every preparation
made to give a suitable reception to the highest dignitary of the Roman
Catholic Church in the United States, and a welcome and congratulation for his successful efforts in behalf of Catholicism in the late Œcumenical Council at Rome, in which he bore a prominent part, and his
safe return to his Archbishopric. Let others speak as they may, it is
certain that the Roman Catholics exhibit a more perfect enthusiasm
and veneration for their Church and its Priests than perhaps members
of any other creed, for this was shown in the demonstration of Thursday.
Old and young, rich and poor, high and low, white and colored, turned
out *en masse* to welcome their Archbishop; and this vast throng of
moving, breathing humanity was further swelled by large accessions of
people of other creeds, whom curiosity had called out to witness one of
those brilliant and imposing pageants for which the Catholics are re-
markable. The day dawned clear and beautiful, and the air was as
balmy as on a day in spring.

As early as nine o'clock the vicinity of the Baltimore depot was
thronged with a miscellaneous crowd of human beings, each and every
one anxious to secure a position from which to see the Archbishop as
he alighted from the cars. Every coign of vantage was made use of—

the fences, the house-tops, and the neighboring windows. A little later the different Societies, Sodalities, and other organizations of the Catholic congregations of the District, arrived one after another and took up their positions.

ARRIVAL OF THE TRAIN.

As the 9.30 train arrived the excitement became intense, and it was with difficulty that the crowd were prevented from injuring each other in their eager rush forward. After a few minutes had elapsed,

THE ARCHBISHOP WITH HIS SUITE,

(consisting of Fathers WALTER, BOYLE, and DOUGHERTY; Father HENCHY, President of Loyola College; Father GAITLEY, of St. Patrick's Church; Father VOLTZ, of St. Joseph's, the Washington Committee, and the following citizens of Baltimore, who acted as a guard of honor: Gen. JOS. H. BRENT, Dr. ROBERT H. GOLDSMITH, JAS. W. JENKINS, MICHAEL J. KELLY, SAMUEL H. ADAMS, JOSEPH S. HEUISLER, Col. FRANK X. WARD, JOHN WICKERSHAM, CHAS. B. TIERNAN, JOHN B. TIDY, Jr., FRANCIS WM. DAMMANN, and Judge BOLIVAR D. DANELS, the latter acting as chairman, together with the Clergy of this city,) emerged from the front door of the depot. His Grace entered a barouche in waiting, to which were attached four beautiful bay horses splendidly caparisoned, the Marine Band stationed there in the meantime playing "Hail to the Chief."

When the Archbishop had taken his seat in the barouche,

THE PROCESSION

moved off in the following order:

Mounted Police, under Lieutenant Johnson.

Chief Marshal, JOHN H. GODDARD, and Assistants, A. A. MARR, and J. E. MALLETT.

St. Cecilia's Band.

Assistant Chief Marshal, T. D. Daly.

The Young Catholics' Friend Society of Georgetown.

The Catholic Total Abstinence Society, and Male Members of Holy Trinity Congregation.

Band.

The Male Members of St. Patrick's Congregation, James Keleher, Marshal, in charge; M. Welch, Assistant.

St. Patrick's Total Abstinence Society, numbering about 80. J. J. Carrigan, Marshal.

The Hibernia Benevolent Society, about 100 members. D. Shannon, Marshal; Messrs. Welch and Tracy, Assistants.

St. Peter's Temperance Society, and the Male Members of St. Peter's Congregation.

The Male Members of St. Matthew's Congregation, about 250 in number. M. Green, Marshal in charge; L. J. O'Toole and Dr. L. J. Draper, Assistants.

Assistant Chief Marshal George E. Kirk.

Band.

St. Dominick's Total Abstinence Society, and the Male Members of St. Dominick's Congregation.

St. Mary's and St. Joseph's, P. May and J. B. Ruth, Marshals, with B. Grier, H. Ruppert, John Ruppert, M. May, H. Kramer, and M. Ruth, Assistants; Washington Germania Band, (Weber's.) The flag of the Pope.

St. Joseph's Beneficial Society, Marshaled by John Kaiser, numbering 100 members, headed by a banner with painting of saint, with date of organization, October 13, 1846.

St. Bonifacius' Society, Marshaled by H. Nairn, with banner bearing portrait of saint.

St. Michael's Society, numbering about 100 members, Marshaled by B. Neff and John Gettinger, headed by blue silk banner with portrait of saint and date of organization, September 29, 1869.

Esputa's Band, John Moran, Marshal; H. G. and W. F. Tyson, Assistants.

Sodality of St. Aloysius', numbering about 300, Marshaled by T. Stewart; headed by a beautiful white silk banner bearing on the front a portrait of the saint, inscribed, "Erected under the patronage of St. Aloysius Gonzaga, August, 1860;" on the reverse, representation of the Virgin bruising the serpent.

St. Aloysius' Temperance Society, numbering about 100; Marshaled by Messrs. George Savage, Fitz, Carmody, and Batson. A fine banner headed this body, on the white front the inscription, "St. Aloysius' Beneficial Society, organized November 17, 1866," and on the green reverse a representation of Father Mathew speaking on temperance, with the inscription, "We practice what we preach."

The Male Members of the Immaculate Conception Congregation, James Forsyth, Marshal, in charge; C. P. Clarke, Jerome McManus, M. J. Hurley, C. A. Mullaly, M. Dorant, and M. Mulloy, Assistants.

The Sodality of the Blessed Virgin Mary, 110 members.

The Male Members of St. Stephen's Congregation, Thomas E. Waggaman, Marshal, in charge; James Carol and John F. Curran, Assistants.

St. Stephen's Educational Society, numbering about 100 members, James McKenna, Marshal.

St. Stephen's Total Abstinence Society, 65 in number, William Ryan, Marshal, who had a fine silk banner, and wore green ribbon badges pinned to the left lappel of the coat, with a large gold star.

The division of Colored Catholics was Marshaled by W. H. Smith, assisted by T. E. Coakley and T. B. Bowie.

St. Martin's Beethoven Band, Marshaled by A. Queen, led the division.

Next came the Catholic Benevolent Society, numbering about 100, with beautiful silk banner, having on the front a representation of two male attendants waiting on an invalid, and on the reverse the inscription, "Presented to the Catholic Benevolent Society by the ladies of Washington, January 3, 1867."

Blessed Peter Claver Society, of Georgetown, numbering 43 members, having a fine banner, with a painting with the words of Philippians, ii., 2, and on the reverse, organized 1865, and the words, "A brother that is helped by his brother is like a strong city," Prov. xxiii., 19, and a fine flag.

St. Peter's Beneficial Society, numbering 147 members, with banner, headed by the South Washington Band, led by Joseph Lee.

King's Band.

St. Martin's Society, headed by a fine banner, with a representation of the Virgin, embroidered.

Blessed Martin's Educational Society, numbering 100 members, with banner having on the front the name, month, date of organization, 1868.

The Marshals of these Associations were the following: W. H Wheeler, J. F. Jackson, H. Chandler, W. T. Bergerman, C. H. M. Wood, R. Hatton, E. Fletcher, A. B. Thomas, John Mitchell, D. Sprigg, F. Hawkins, Thomas Delany.

The Marine Band.

The Young Catholics' Friends Society, as a guard of honor to the Most Reverend Archbishop.

The first carriage contained Hon. Messrs. R. T. MERRICK and J. CARROLL BRENT, and was followed by the barouche in which were seated the Archbishop, Rev. Dr. WHITE and Judge DANELS. Then came a long line of carriages with the Clergy of this city and Baltimore, the Committee of Reception, Baltimore Visiters and others.

THE ROUTE OF THE PROCESSION

was along C street to Sixth, up Sixth to F, along F to Fourteenth, up Fourteenth to New York avenue, down New York and along Pennsylvania avenue to Seventeenth street, up Seventeenth to H street, and thence along H to St. Matthew's Church.

Along the line of march crowds of spectators were gathered on the sidewalks and thronged the windows and doorways, and even the house-tops were brought into requisition. On the south portico of the Patent Office a large multitude had assembled, whom the Archbishop saluted by courteously lifting his hat. The male and female orphans, dressed in their neat uniforms, were drawn up in parallel lines upon the grassy slope of St. Patrick's Church lot, and waved their white handkerchiefs unceasingly, presenting a fine effect. In fine, but for the absence of the military, the occasion would compare favorably with inauguration day, in point of numbers present and enthusiasm manifested.

ST. MATTHEW'S CHURCH.

The vestibule of the church had been beautifully decorated with flowers and evergreens, large festoons and wreaths being tastefully en-twined around the columns, an arch elaborately decorated with rare exotics being sprung between the centre columns in front of the main entrance, and surmounted with a large gilt mitre and cross, emblemati-cal of the distinguished rank of the Archbishop in the Church. Over the cornice surmounting the columns, a beautiful floral cross, relieved with handsome evergreen wreaths, hung suspended, and attracted many admiring comments. The interior of the church had been appropriately decorated, the altar effectively and elaborately arranged with innumer-able lights and boquets of aromatic flowers, and on the left of the space within the sanctuary a magnificent throne had been raised, covered with a canopy of purple and gold, for the reception of the Archbishop upon his arrival.

THE CROWD.

From an early hour the people began to arrive at the front of the church, and gradually the entire street became packed with living beings from Fourteenth to Fifteenth street, up and down Fifteenth street, and excitedly pressing in upon the space which the police had endeavored to preserve for the ceremonies when the procession should arrive. At times the street was so jammed with men, women and children, that the H street cars were compelled to stop and wait a long time for space to be cleared for them to pass. The press of the crowd here was so great that it was almost impossible for the mounted and foot-police to keep anything like order. The church doors were kept closed.

ARRIVAL OF THE PROCESSION.

The arrival of the procession only augmented the difficulties of the situation, the immense throng being so packed together as to render it

literally impracticable to move them. Finally, after some delay, the
carriage containing the Archbishop and his escort arrived in front of
the church, and the distinguished visiter was escorted to the door. He
at once entered the church, and was dressed in his robes of office.
After a few moments he reappeared at the door, when

THE ADDRESS OF WELCOME

was delivered by Mr. Brent. He said:

"Upon appointment, and in behalf of the Catholic laity of Washington and Georgetown, I have the honor and signal privilege, unworthily
though that honor be bestowed, of extending, in behalf of your flock,
their hearty and sincere welcome, on this your first visit to this portion
of your diocese since your return from the Holy City.

"The display on this occasion, and the crowds that you have seen
file up before you, the enthusiasm of those who witnessed your trium-
phant procession through the avenues and streets of the metropolis, all
render words on my part unnecessary to impress upon you the high
esteem, the veneration which they feel for the dignity of the Prelate,
and the sentiments of affection, of warm, and hearty attachment they
have for the virtues, the graces, and the merits of the man. It seems
to me, therefore, most venerable and beloved Archbishop, that on this
auspicious occasion we, the Catholic laity of the District of Columbia,
have more reason, more causes for congratulation and for rejoicing on
this legal Thanksgiving Day of the country, in consequence of having
met you in good health and with increased prospects of future usefulness in the Church in which you are an ornament, and of which you
are the champion, in having your presence with us on this occasion, to
give us your benediction, and to cheer us with the words we need from
your lips.

"I therefore, in behalf of this assembled multitude, greet you, Most
Reverend Prelate, from their hearts, as from my own, in those most
welcome words, 'All hail to our good and gracious Archbishop, on his
visit to us on this memorable occasion.'"

RESPONSE OF ARCHBISHOP SPALDING.

The Archbishop then responded as follows:

"I thank you, Mr. BRENT, as the organ of this immense assemblage,
for your cordial welcome. I am sure from what I have seen, that you
have but reëchoed those kindly feelings which have prompted them all
—the laity with the clergy—to welcome me on this occasion. I feel
deeply gratified for all this kindness, though I deem myself unworthy
of it. The only thing I can plead is, that I have, I think, honestly
wished in general to do my duty, and to promote the spiritual welfare

of the large and most respectable flock which Almighty God has committed to my charge. But there is one, Mr. Brent, Catholics of this great metropolis of the greatest nation on the face of God's earth, (applause,) there is one who is worthy of all our love, of all our veneration, and, I may add, of all our sympathies. One who now is really a prisoner; he to whom two hundred million Christians look up with reverence and with love; a prisoner on that little territory, that little District of Columbia, the little neutral Holy soil, which he held and administered for the benefit of all, that is, of two hundred million of Christians. He has been imprisoned under such circumstances; an outrage fully as great as if this District of Columbia, which belongs to the United States of America, were seized upon, and the President imprisoned by a neighboring State, which happened to find it to its convenience to possess itself of this territory. Pius IX. merits all our love, merits all our sympathy, and I trust that as in Baltimore, so also in this great metropolis, we, his spiritual children, looking only to the freedom of his intercourse, as their spiritual father, with the great body of Christians, will assert the principles of that freedom which cannot be guaranteed him, unless he be independent of every other sovereignty, uninfluenced by any of the complications of modern politics. Now all Europe is in commotion, and, dearly beloved of the laity, I am sure that you will unite with my beloved and venerable brethren of the Clergy, with all of us, in giving such expression to that feeling as your faith and your good hearts may prompt. Of course, in this there is no interference intended with the political relations of foreign or neighboring States. All we want for Pius IX is to have him free and untrammeled. That is all we ask. (Applause.) I thank you again, dearly beloved, and hope that God will bless you and your families, increase your numbers as He has increased your churches, from one to eleven, within a very few years, within the memory of some who are now living. God bless you!"

At the conclusion of the Most Reverend Archbishop's remarks, the ceremonial set forth by the Church for the reception of an Archbishop was then proceeded with. Rev. CHARLES I. WHITE, D. D., pastor of St. Matthew's Church, on behalf of the Clergy, conducted the ceremony. The Archbishop was escorted up the aisle, preceded by the incense-bearers, and, entering the sanctuary, seated himself upon the Episcopal throne. While the procession was marching to the sanctuary the orchestra played, with fine effect, the *"Marche Du Sacre,"* from Meyerbeer's "Prophete." The Reverend Clergy who accompanied the Archbishop took the stations assigned them in the sanctuary, and the doors of the edifice were then opened to the vast assemblage congregated without, or such of them as were so fortunate to crowd inside, who filled all the available space between its walls.

The choir, accompanied by the grand orchestra and organ, and led by Mr. L. E. Gannon, then sang from Haydn's oratorio of the "Creation" the chorus entitled "The Heavens are telling the Glory of God," the solo parts being acceptably rendered by Mr. Widney, Miss Juliana May, and Miss Reynolds.

Rev. Dr. WHITE then addressed the Archbishop as follows:

ADDRESS OF DR. WHITE.

"Most Reverend Archbishop, in the name of the Reverend Clergy and the Laity of the Catholic Church in the District of Columbia, I extend to you a cordial welcome on your return to the archdiocese over whose spiritual interests you preside. It has been the custom of enlightened nations in every age to hail with joy and festivity the victor re-appearing among them after the dangers of the battle-field, and to manifest by a patriotic demonstration their grateful appreciation of the heroism displayed and the triumphs achieved for their country's welfare. How much more must a Christian people rise to the enthusiasm of the occasion, when they again behold among them the chief pastor of the flock, after the labors and trials undergone, with distinguished zeal and success, for their spiritual and eternal interests! It is not for us, Most Reverend Sir, to pronounce upon the merit and efficiency of the part which you took in the deliberations of that august assembly of prelates convened in the Eternal City from every region of the globe to proclaim the faith of Christ, and to provide for its increased influence among men by the enactment of salutary laws. It is not for the children to sit in judgment upon the father; but it is our privilege at least to congratulate ourselves and the Catholic body at large in having been represented in that venerable and imposing synod by a Prelate whose talents, learning, and zeal entitled him, by the common consent of the Christian world, to be considered as one of the brightest ornaments of the Catholic hierarchy and one of the staunchest pillars of the Church. The honor which you enjoyed by so prominent an association with that galaxy of intelligence and virtue which shone forth in the Œcumenical Council we feel reflected upon ourselves, for it reminds us of our birthright as Christians, that in entering into fellowship with the mystical body of Christ, we did not become members of any human organization, liable to error, corruption, and decay, but were affiliated to that Church which is immortal because it is infallible—a Church founded by the Son of God made man, with which he promised to remain all days to the end of time, and against which the gates of hell shall never prevail—

possessing a divine life, and guided in her external action by the unerring decisions of her supreme pastor, the Bishop of Rome. She prospers alike under the smiles of friends and the persecution of enemies. As loyal children we rejoice in her joys and sympathize in her trials. And now that her august ruler, the magnanimous Pius IX, has been assailed by the shafts of the enemy, and in the desecrated name of liberty and progress has been despoiled of his temporal dominion, and stripped of that independence which is necessary for the free exercise of his exalted functions, and for untrammeled influence with his two hundred millions of children throughout the globe, the whole Catholic world feels the outrage which has been committed against him, and through him against religion and society. He, in his spiritual character and temporal headship, was the only subsisting illustration in modern times of the normal state of Christian society ; that is, of the perfect accord between the natural and supernatural order. But an impious hand has for a moment overthrown this model structure.

" On this occasion, therefore, which reminds us that you, Most Reverend Sir, and your illustrious colleagues in the Œcumenical Council, have been compelled to suspend your proceedings, by the same sacrilegious violence and wholesale robbery that have invaded the Papal territory, we cannot but lift our voice, with one accord, and in earnest tones, to protest against the iniquity ; and we deem the present a fitting moment, with your permission, to make a public declaration of the sentiments which the gravity of the aforementioned circumstances must naturally inspire. But, Most Reverend Archbishop, allow us to assure you, that whether you are here, surrounded by a loyal and affectionate flock, giving life and energy to every department of your spiritual administration, or absent from us on a wider theatre of usefulness, opposing yourself as a wall of brass against the latitudinarianism and infidelity of the age, you will always be the object of our profound veneration and devoted attachment."

REPLY OF ARCHBISHOP SPALDING.

The Archbishop, in reply, said :

" Rev. Dr. WHITE and venerable members of the Clergy of the District, I return you my most heartfelt thanks for your cordial greeting on my return. I thank you for your, I fear, too partial estimate of the little that I was able to do in the Œcumenical Council. True, I was placed in positions of considerable responsibility by the partial opinion of the Sovereign Pontiff and by the votes of a majority among nearly eight hundred of my colleagues assembled, but I was only one of many, and I felt then less than I ever felt in all my life. When a man is one among so many, when among the Archbishops he ranks No. 131, as I did, of course it makes us feel how small we are. One never feels so little, for instance, as when he finds himself in the centre of London or Paris.

"I thank you, Venerable Brethren, and I hope that, as our relations have always been very good, that they will continue to become even more intimate, and that we will all continue to labor in unison for the greater glory of God and the salvation of souls.

"I will add to what I said at the door, lest there should be any misunderstanding, one reflection; that is, in reference to what you were kind enough to say about the present position of the Sovereign Pontiff. I wish to put this case: Supposing that the people of three or four States, or one State—Maryland even, or Virginia—should come here and seize the District of Columbia, and throw a guard around the White-House grounds, and say to the President, 'Oh, you are free, perfectly free; you can write or correspond, but all such correspondence has to pass through our hands.' To the Departments—say the Post Office, 'You are free, but recollect we have to superintend your freedom; you can communicate with the whole of the United States, but all that you send must be subject to our inspection. We will disperse your Congress, as that is of no use.' That is exactly what those pretended lovers of liberty in Italy have done. They dispersed the Congress of Christendom, composed of nearly eight hundred Bishops, drove them home, and imprisoned the President. And, then, they think that he is simple enough to believe that he is free. Free, with a mounted guard all around the Vatican Palace. Free, when he has not been able to go out into the city once since the 20th of September, for fear of being insulted. He walks only in his own garden. Such is the liberty left to the man to whom 200,000,000 of Christian men, from every quarter of the globe, look up for spiritual advice and guidance. I thank you again, with all my heart, for this unexpected and splendid, and certainly very cordial demonstration."

Upon the conclusion of the Archbishop's reply, Rev. Dr. WHITE announced that they would now proceed to organize the meeting for the purpose of passing such resolutions as the occasion required.

On motion by L. F. CLARK, Esq., L. JOHNSON, Esq., was elected President, and Messrs. EDWARD GIMMO, WILLIAM FORSYTH, SERAPHIM MASI, W. H. NEWMAN, JOHN T. CASSELL, C. V. KINE, J. Q. McGILL, RUDOLPH EICHORN, Vice Presidents, and JOHN F. ENNIS, Secretary.

Reverend Father BOYLE, pastor of St. Peter's Church, then read the resolutions expressive of the sense of the meeting at the expulsion of the Pope from his temporal power in Rome.

They were unanimously adopted. They were the same as those adopted in Baltimore.

The Most Reverend Archbishop then said :

" With renewed thanks, my beloved children of the laity and venerable Clergy, the exercises are now terminated. God bless you."

The grand " Hallelujah Chorus," from Handel's Oratorio of the " Mesiah," was then sung by the choir, after which the congregation dispersed.

While the exercises were in progress in the church, a meeting was organized outside, and the protest and resolutions were read to the assembled multitude by Mr. Frank McNerhany, and unanimously adopted.

After the arrival of the Archbishop at Georgetown College the gentlemen from Baltimore, who had come hither as a guard of honor, were invited to Carroll Hall to partake of an entertainment prepared by the Washington Reception Committee. John F. Ennis, Esq., presided at the entertainment. Toasts were offered, in response to which speeches were delivered by Judge Daniels, Dr. Goldsmith, Rev. Father Dougherty, Mr. Kelly, and others of Baltimore, and by Mr. Ennis and Father Walter and Father Kane, of this city. The Baltimore guests left for their homes on the six o'clock train.

The decorations of St. Matthew's Church were designed by Mr. L. F. Clark, and executed by Mr. S. S. Parker and a corps of workmen. The ladies of St. Matthew's deserve the highest credit for the assistance they rendered in preparing the church, &c.

ARCHBISHOP SPALDING'S RECEPTION AT GEORGETOWN COLLEGE.

At the close of the ceremonies in Washington, the Archbishop was attended to the College by the Committee of Reception of the Washington Catholic Laity, and by many of the Clergy, and also by the gentlemen of his escort from Baltimore. A numerous company then assembled at dinner, at the college, at half past two.

In the evening, the students tendered their reception in their refectory, a large hall adorned for the occasion with floral ornaments, banners, &c. Over the platform for the speakers was a long Latin inscription of welcome, in the style called " Lapidary," a handsome painting of the Papal arms being near it on one side, and another of the American arms on the other. On the entrance of the Archbishop, with the Faculty of the college, the students rose to their feet, and welcomed him with great applause. Courteously acknowledging their salute, he took a seat in front of the platform, and the exercises began with the perfomance of a piece of instrumental music, the performers being students, under the direction of Professor Föertoch. Music, either vocal or instrumental, followed the delivery of each piece on the programme, and with an execution that did the performers great credit.

Mr. Denis Sheridan, of Cumberland, Md., then arose and delivered the salutatory, as follows:

"Most Reverend Archbishop, it is my happy privilege on this occasion to bid you welcome to Georgetown College, in the name of her faculty and students, and to congratulate you on having escaped all the perils of an ocean voyage.

"A year ago you left us at the call of the Sovereign Pontiff, to assist at the august Council of the Church Militant; and the honorable and important duties assigned you in its deliberations, besides being well-deserved tributes to your zeal and devotion in the cause of our holy religion, are also a source of pride and gratification to us.

"The events which preceded your return, and which indeed caused it, have cast a shadow over the joy we experience to-day. The breaking out of the war in France has given a long-desired opportunity to the enemies of the holy Church to attack the temporal power of the Pope, and wrest from his sway the last remnant of his territory. Only too well have they succeeded in their infamous designs.

"Rome has fallen. The solemn session of the Œcumenical Council has been interrupted. The grave and Reverend Prelates who composed it have been dispersed, and the Vicar of Christ imprisoned in his palace, while the temples and shrines of his Divine Master are outraged and profaned by his enemies. In the sorrow with which these evils have filled our hearts, it is some solace to believe with the Holy Father himself, that they are but the misfortunes of an hour, which God has permitted in order to try the devotion of His children, and that the Church, refined and purified by the fires of persecution, will come forth from the struggle more glorious than ever. As we cannot approach nor even communicate directly with the Holy Father in his afflictions, it is some satisfaction to us to declare our dutiful love and devotion to his sacred cause and his august person in your presence, as his worthiest representative. In conclusion, Most Reverend Sir, whilst we pray that God may add many years to the life you have devoted to His service, we beg of you, as a special favor, that when you stand face to face with the venerable Pius IX., you will tell him of the sentiments of filial love and sympathy that animate his children of Georgetown College."

Mr. Sheridan was followed by A. W. Madigan, of Maine, with an address in Latin verse, "*Pastor Nauta.*"

Thos. A. Badeaux, of Louisiana, then recited a poem in French, "*Au Concile Œcuménique,*" followed by an address in German, "*Der Protest von Genf,*" from Master Julius von Sacks, of New York. To the latter succeeded Master George W. Douglas, of Washington, D. C., with the recitation of a poem, in English, which, like all the other addresses, was excellently rendered.

The concluding address was delivered by Mr. G. Gordon Posey, of Mississippi, who said :

"Most Reverend Sir : Perhaps to some it may seem presumptuous in us, mere students and striplings, to attempt, even by way of protest, the discussion of events, which, by their magnitude and extent, embrace the interests, not only of Catholicism, but of the world. But we consider that we are members of one great family, and that when the head and father of this our family is menaced with destruction, or treated with contempt and disrespect, not only have we a right, but we are bound in duty to raise our voices, feeble though they be, to swell the solemn protest rising from

TWO HUNDRED MILLION CATHOLIC HEARTS

throughout the world, against the dastardly, unprovoked and unwarrantable outrages inflicted upon our Holy Father, the Pope, by the minions of fanaticism and infidelity under the leadership of Victor Emmanuel. And of all the expressions of sympathy now going up to the Holy Father we feel confident that not the least cheering is the profession of strong faith and earnest attachment offered by the Catholic youth, for it shows to him and to the world that the rising generation is not wholly imbued with the poison of infidelity and indifferentism, but that they cling with unswerving devotion to the traditions of their fathers and the tenets of their faith. Therefore, the students of this College, in mass meeting assembled, have adopted the following preamble and resolutions, which they submit to the approval of your Grace, with the request that you will forward them to his Holiness, together with this little offering."

He then read the resolutions, which had been adopted at the meeting of the students on the Thursday of the previous week, Mr. Posey having been on that occasion delegated by vote as the reader on this occasion. The resolutions are as follows :

Whereas it is absolutely necessary to the right direction of a religious body that its head be left wholly untrammelled and free in its actions ; and

Whereas we regard any departure from this principle as an outrage on the rights of conscience ; and

Whereas we have beheld with sorrow and indignation the forcible seizure of the Papal States by the Italian Government, in violation of the plighted faith of treaties and of the laws of nations ; therefore, be it

Resolved, That we, the students of Georgetown College, District of Columbia, in mass meeting assembled, do hereby enter our solemn protest against this system of spoliation and robbery inaugurated by the

Italian Government, and in particular by its unscrupulous ruler, Victor Emmanuel.

Resolved, That we resent, as an indignity to ourselves as Catholics, the sacrilegious outrages practised on the person of the Holy Father.

Resolved, That we regard the action of the usurping authorities in closing the colleges of Rome as indicative of a spirit hostile to the cause of education and progress.

Resolved, That we invite the students of all the Catholic institutions of this country to join us in tendering to the Pope the expression of our deepest sympathy for his affliction, and of our unshaken devotion to the holy cause ; and be it further

Resolved, That whereas actions are of more importance than words, we hereby determine to raise a fund for the relief of the temporal necessities of the Holy Father, and we hope that the youth of America will co-operate with us in this good work.

Mr. Posey then descended from the stage and placed in the Archbishop's hands an engrossed copy of the resolutions, and an enclosure containing $500, of which sum, $290 were contributed by the students themselves, the whole to be remitted to the Holy Father. Mr. Posey then remarked that he had a request to make of the Archbishop, which it would not be difficult for him to accede to. It was, with the approval of the faculty, to grant the students a holiday on Saturday.

"Granted !" replied the Archbishop promptly, at which there was great cheering on the part of the boys.

The Archbishop then arose, and addressing the speakers said :

" I beg, young gentlemen, to return you my most heartfelt thanks for the kindly feeling you have shown, and the truly Catholic manner in which you have expressed your sentiments on this occasion. Speaking here in the name of the faculty and your fellow students, you have acquitted yourselves eloquently in four different languages. The faculty knew what they were about when they selected you. For what you so courteously said of myself I thank you sincerely ; but there is only one thing in which I can claim to be worthy of your commendation, and that is that I have worked with good will in a good and holy cause. For the Holy Father I thank you most sincerely. It is beautiful to hear such sentiments welling up spontaneously from young and pure hearts. Your speaking in four languages makes this a sort of miniature council. In the great Council at Rome there were those who spoke some seventy different languages, and it is an illustration of the wisdom and sagacity of the Catholic Church in establishing Latin as the language of the Church ; for at this great Council, where so many dialects were represented, there was but one tongue spoken, as there was but one heart and one faith. I had the pleasure, if it may be called a pleasure in such hot weather as we sometimes had in Rome, of hearing four hundred speeches in Latin ; some long, most of them eloquent, though seldom trimmed with figures of rhetoric ; for it was expected that they should confine themselves strictly to statements of principles, facts, and ecclesiastical precedents. It was hard to make any appreciable impression otherwise ; the grave and Reverend Signors were very hard to please, and occasionally they were a little annoyed by speakers who indulged in flourishes of rhetoric instead of facts. There, where seventy languages were spoken, all were of one heart ; and may you, my dear children, be of one heart, and the worthy sentiments you have expressed be matured and rooted so firmly that all the storms of your after life may not eradicate them. Again I thank you, most especially for our Holy Father, Pius the Ninth. No one who sees him but must love him. So pure and unsullied in his life, that none, not even his most bitter enemies, have ever assailed it. His mild and saintly character has given him a world-wide reputation. I thank you for him, and will repeat to him what you have said, and will send him your generous offering ; and it will make his old heart glad that so many of the rising generation here in the District of Columbia, where all sections of our great and glorious country are represented, have united in this offering, showing their sympathy and love for him, and their attachment to the Church of which he is the visible head. I will now give to you all, his blessing, which he authorized me to do on all such occasions, and I have no doubt that when I receive an answer to the message I will send him from you, he will again transmit his benediction."

The assemblage then kneeled and received from the Archbishop, the PAPAL BENEDICTION ; after which they arose, and a piece by the band closed the exercises.

www.ingramcontent.com/pod-product-compliance
Lightning Source LLC
Chambersburg PA
CBHW021550270326
41930CB00008B/1450